ST—————L
E—————

LEARN IT, TRY IT!

Tammy Enz

Raintree is an imprint of Capstone Global Library Limited, a company incorporated in England and Wales having its registered office at 264 Banbury Road, Oxford, OX2 7DY – Registered company number: 6695582

www.raintree.co.uk
myorders@raintree.co.uk

Edited by Mandy Robbins
Designed by Steve Mead
Picture research by Kelli Lageson
Production by Laura Manthe
Originated by Capstone Global Library Limited
Printed and bound in India

ISBN 978 1 474 74063 0 (hardback)
21 20 19 18 17
10 9 8 7 6 5 4 3 2 1

ISBN 978 1 474 74067 8 (paperback)
22 21 20 19 18
10 9 8 7 6 5 4 3 2 1

British Library Cataloguing in Publication Data
A full catalogue record for this book is available from the British Library.

Acknowledgements
We would like to thank the following for permission to reproduce photographs: Capstone Studio: Karon Dubke, cover (bottom right), back cover, 6 (top and bottom), 7 (top and bottom), 14, 15 (top, middle, bottom), 18 (top and bottom), 19 (top, middle, bottom), 24 (top and bottom), 25 (left and right), 30 (top and bottom), 31 (top, middle, bottom), 34 (top and bottom), 35 (left, middle, right), 42 (top and bottom), 43 (top, middle, bottom), 44 (top and bottom), 45; Dreamstime: Per Björkdahl, cover (bottom left); Shutterstock: Aleph Studio, 10, Andrew Zarivny, 9, AndreyCherkasov, 12, Anna Bolotnikova, 27 (bottom), Checubus, 28, Chombosan, 40, Christopher PB, 41 (back), chuyuss, 37 (inset), Eric Fahrner, 11, Guzel Studio, 23 (bottom left), iamlukyeee, 36, Jim Parkin, 27 (top), Keith A Frith, 21, Lukasz Pajor, 16, Mikhail Olykainen, 20, Mmaxer, 39, Multistock, 22, 23 (top right), Nelson Charette Photo, 38, Radiokafka, 32, Renata Sedmakova, cover (top right), Richard Thornton, 28 (inset), rickyd, 26, Santi Rodriguez, 5 (inset), Sean Pavone, 41 (top inset), superjoseph, 33, twoandonebuilding, 4, YuSev, cover (top left)

Illustrations by Oxford design and Illustrators

Design elements: Shutterstock

CONTENTS

CHAPTER 1

WHAT IS STRUCTURAL ENGINEERING?

Have you ever travelled in a tunnel through a mountain or under city streets? Have you ever gazed at a skyscraper swaying in the wind? Have you peered over the edge of a bridge? Then you've taken a look at structural engineering.

A structure is anything designed to **resist** or support a force or load. Structural engineers usually design buildings and bridges. They also work on projects such as aeroplane bodies and equipment supports.

Structural engineering is an ancient science. Ancient builders may not have had today's methods to calculate forces and test materials. But they understood the concepts. The results of their understanding are seen in ancient pyramids and arched bridges. Many are still standing after thousands of years.

The parts of a structure are often easy to see. In a bridge each steel beam or concrete slab is part of the structure. The structure of a building is often harder to see. The beams, columns and braces that support it can be hidden under flooring or behind walls. But each piece has a purpose.

FACT

All structures use the same structural engineering principles. The Guggenheim Museum in Spain looks like a complex structure. But its design principles are the same as those used in a simple house.

The Pont du Gard in France is 2,000 years old. The Romans built the structure to deliver water. Today it is used as a bridge.

resist force that opposes or slows the motion of another force or object

PROJECT 1

EXPERIMENT WITH STRUCTURAL SHAPES

Did you know that the shapes of structures and their parts affects their strength? Test out some shapes to see for yourself.

MATERIALS

ROASTING TIN

SMALL BUCKET OF SAND

CLEAR TAPE

SEVERAL PAPERBACK BOOKS

6 SHEETS OF POSTER BOARD MEASURING 22 X 28 CENTIMETRES (8.5 X 11 INCHES)

STEPS

1   Fold a piece of poster board into thirds along the longer side. Unfold to make a triangular tube. Tape the edges together.

2   Make a fold 4 centimetres (1.5 inches) from each edge of the longer side of another piece of poster board. Unfold and carefully bend and tape the edges together to form a dome-shaped tube.

3   Fold another piece into a square-shaped tube. Tape the edges together.

4   Repeat Steps 1 to 3 to make two of each shape.

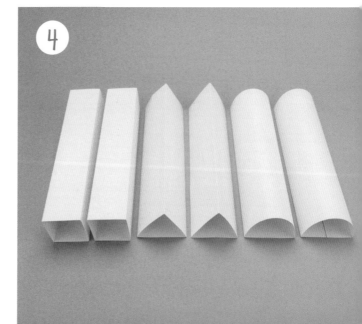

4

5 Lay the square tubes on their sides next to each other. One at a time, stack books on top until the tubes flatten.

6 Repeat the experiment with the other tubes. Which of the shapes can support the most books?

7 Now place one of the square tubes on its side in a roasting tin. Slowly and evenly pour sand around the tube until it is nearly covered.

8 Repeat step 7 with the other tubes. Which tube keeps its shape best? What if you stack the books on top too?

WHAT HAPPENED?

In the first experiment, it's likely that the triangle held the most weight. A triangle is one of the strongest structural shapes. Its stable angles help to evenly distribute loads to all sides. You'll often see the triangle shape in buildings and bridges. The Burj Khalifa tower in Dubai and the Louvre in Paris are two famous examples.

So why does the dome shape hold up better when buried? A triangle is strong when loaded at its points. But pushing on its sides weakens it. Domes and arches are strong when loads are placed all around them. This is why the arch shape is used for most tunnels.

Challenge

Experiment with the sizes of the structural shapes. Do bigger triangles or domes support more weight? What about smaller ones?

CHAPTER 2

STRUCTURAL FORCES AND MATERIALS

Many of the materials in your house are not structural materials. These include the glass, carpet and plaster that cover walls and floors. The real structure is hidden behind or beneath them. Wood, steel and concrete are commonly used structural materials. They are strong enough to hold up all the weight and forces on a structure.

But materials need more than strength to work well. They also need a little **elasticity**. Elasticity allows something to change shape and return to its original shape. In fact, the secret to a structure's strength is its ability to stretch and bend without breaking.

Different forces cause a structure to change its shape. This includes the weight of people and cars. Blowing wind can also cause changes. Heating or cooling makes structures expand and contract. These changes are called **deflection**. You may not notice it, but it's possible the floor in your home deflects a bit as you walk on it.

THE GOLDEN GATE BRIDGE'S DEFLECTION

The Golden Gate Bridge in San Francisco, California, USA, spans 1.9 kilometres (1.2 miles). Its centre can move up and down 4.9 metres (16 feet) as it heats and cools while traffic crosses it. It also deflects sideways as much as 8.2 metres (27 feet) when the wind blows on it.

elasticity   ability of something to change shape and then return to its original shape

deflection   changes in the shape of a structure

STRUCTURAL LOADS

All structures must support loads. There are two types of loads: dead loads and live loads. Dead loads include a structure's own weight and everything attached to it. Windows and walls are part of a dead load. The dead loads on a structure remain the same.

Structures also carry live loads. These loads are the people and other things that move in and out of a structure. Engineers calculate live loads based on how a structure is used. Buildings used for libraries will hold heavy bookshelves. Warehouses hold hefty boxes. Schools and theatres have many people moving through them. The live loads will be different in each of these cases.

Live loads also include forces from nature. It matters if a structure is built in the snowy Scottish highlands or on a sunny Florida beach. Location influences the engineer's design. Structures in cold regions must hold up under heavy piles of snow. Structures in earthquake zones must resist earth tremors. And all buildings must be designed to resist gusts of wind that push on them.

FACT

Hurricanes are huge forces of destruction. They can slam structures with wind speeds of more than 252 kilometres (157 miles) per hour.

TYPES OF FORCES

Loads cause structures to stretch, bend and twist. Each part of a structure is pushed or pulled differently depending on where it is in the structure. The key to choosing the right part to use in a structure is understanding how forces will affect it. Often, structural parts experience more than one type of force.

You usually can't see parts of structures bending, pulling or twisting. But inside they are experiencing these forces. Loads that squeeze are called **compression** forces. Parts that are compressed become shorter. Try gently squashing a marshmallow. Watch it get shorter. **Tension** forces stretch. Structural parts that are in tension stretch out. Now gently stretch the marshmallow. It will lengthen. Bending forces cause parts to be squeezed on one side and stretched on the other at the same time. **Torsion** forces cause twisting.

Different materials are better at handling different types of forces. Steel works well in tension or in compression. Concrete tends to crack in tension. The position of structural parts matters too. They are strongest where they are thickest. A board is stronger when pushed on its edge than when pushed on its flat face.

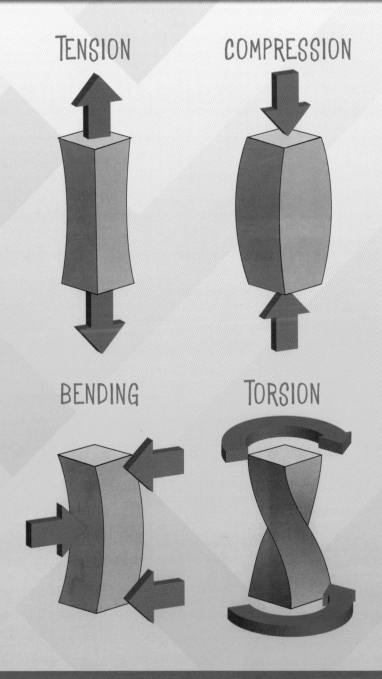

TENSION

COMPRESSION

BENDING

TORSION

compression pushing force

torsion twisting force

tension pulling force

EXPERIMENT WITH MATERIAL STRENGTHS

Try this experiment to compare different material strengths under different loads.

MATERIALS

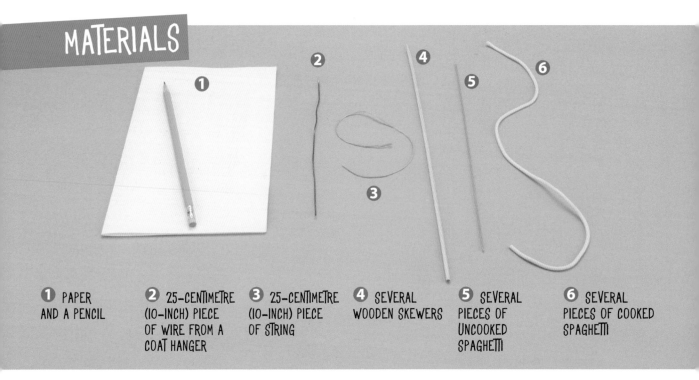

1 PAPER AND A PENCIL

2 25-CENTIMETRE (10-INCH) PIECE OF WIRE FROM A COAT HANGER

3 25-CENTIMETRE (10-INCH) PIECE OF STRING

4 SEVERAL WOODEN SKEWERS

5 SEVERAL PIECES OF UNCOOKED SPAGHETTI

6 SEVERAL PIECES OF COOKED SPAGHETTI

STEPS

1. Use the pencil and paper to draw a table. List the materials in the left-hand column. List the forces across the top, and include a column for "total".

MATERIALS	FORCES				
	Compression	Tension	Bending	Torsion	TOTAL
Wood					
String					
Metal					
Uncooked spaghetti					
Cooked spaghetti					

2 Place a skewer on a flat surface. Use your index finger on each hand to push on each end of the skewer to compress it. Push as hard as you can and see what happens.

3 If the skewer doesn't bend or break at all, give it a score of 10 in your table. If it bends a little, give it a score of 5. Give it a 0 if it breaks easily.

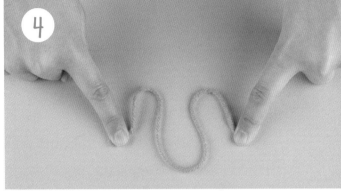

4 Now test the other items for compression using the same pushing force.

5 Next test each material for tension. Hold each end and pull as hard as you can. If the item doesn't break or stretch, give it 10 points. If it stretches a little, give it 5 points. If it breaks immediately, give it a 0.

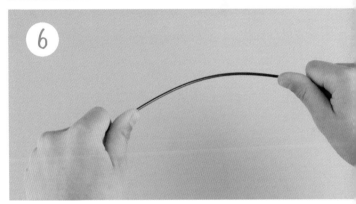

6 Then test each item for bending. Hold each end and push with your thumbs, trying to bend the material. Give scores based on how well each material keeps it shape.

7 Finally, test each material for torsion. Hold each end and twist in opposite directions. Again give scores on how easily the item twists or breaks.

8 Add up the scores for each material and record this in the total column.

WHAT HAPPENED?

This experiment showed why structural engineers use different materials for different parts of a structure. Compare the scores for each of the materials. Which materials received the highest scores?

CHAPTER 3

BRIDGES

Bridges are impressive structures. They do more than carry traffic. They often define a landscape. The Golden Gate Bridge in San Francisco is a well-known symbol of North America's west coast. Tower Bridge in London is one of the most visited sites in Europe. These bridges are beautiful. They're also excellent examples of structural engineering.

Tower Bridge

Each part of a bridge has a purpose. All bridges have below-ground support systems. Giant concrete supports at the bridge ends are called **abutments**. Many bridges also have middle supports called piers. Piers go through the water and rest on the rock below. The part of the bridge cars drive on and people walk on is called the **deck**. But the part you usually notice is the **superstructure**. The superstructure supports the deck. It helps the deck span further between supports.

Bridges are identified by their superstructure type. Short, simple beam bridges are made with steel or concrete beams. But longer decks need the help of arches or trusses. Some of the longest spanning bridges are suspension bridges and cable-stayed bridges. High-tension cables support these types of bridges.

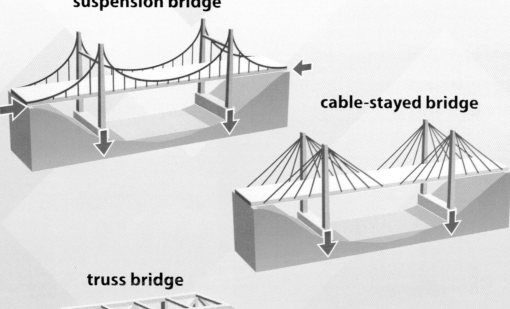

suspension bridge

cable-stayed bridge

truss bridge

arch bridge

Have you ever seen any of these types of bridges?

➡ Direction of force

BUILD AND TEST A CABLE-STAYED BRIDGE

Do you want to see tensioned cables in action? You can build your own cable-stayed bridge with common items from around your home.

MATERIALS

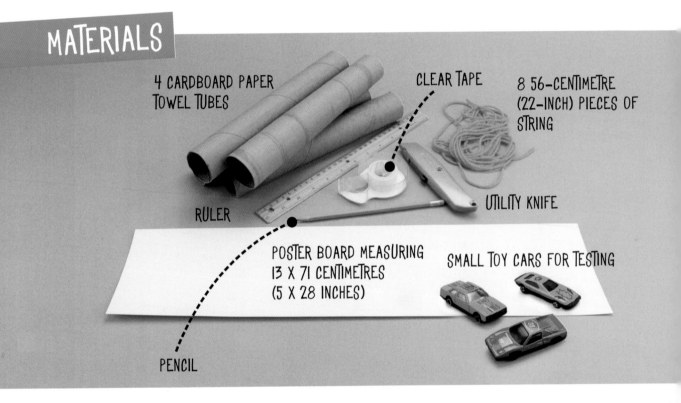

4 CARDBOARD PAPER TOWEL TUBES

CLEAR TAPE

8 56-CENTIMETRE (22-INCH) PIECES OF STRING

RULER

UTILITY KNIFE

POSTER BOARD MEASURING 13 X 71 CENTIMETRES (5 X 28 INCHES)

SMALL TOY CARS FOR TESTING

PENCIL

STEPS

1 Mark a line 8 centimetres (3 inches) from one end of each tube. Ask an adult to help you use the utility knife. Make a slit halfway through each tube at each mark.

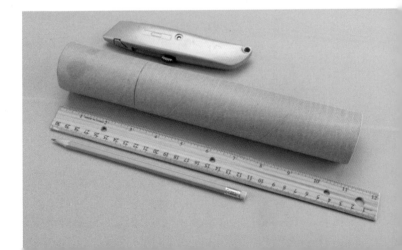

2   Measure and mark a line 20 centimetres (8 inches) from each end of the poster board.

3   Slide the poster board into the slits on the tubes at each end of your marks. This makes the bridge deck. Make sure the 8-centimetre (3-inch) sections of the tubes are placed at the bottom.

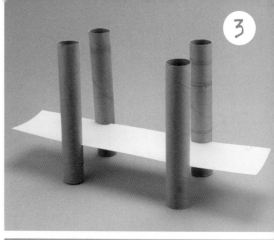

4   Place the bridge on a flat surface and tape down the bottom of each tube.

5   Load the bridge with cars one at a time until the deck begins to sag.

6   Remove the cars. Ask an adult to use the knife to make a 1-centimetre (0.5-inch) slit on the top of the tubes on each side. The slits should be parallel to the bridge deck.

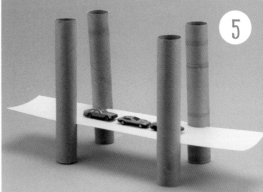

7   Slide two strings into each slit. Make sure they are centred on the slit.

8   Measure and mark 6 centimetres (2.5 inches) from each side of each tube on the deck. Tape one end of a string at each of these marks under the deck.

9   Measure and mark 13 centimetres (5 inches) from each side of each tube. Tape one end of a string to each of these marks under the deck.

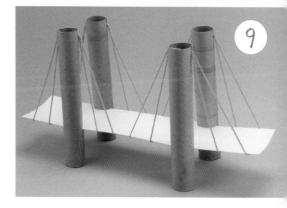

10 Test the bridge deck with cars again. How many cars can it hold now?

WHAT HAPPENED?

The bridge with strings holds more cars. Why? The cables transfer the deck loads to the support columns.

Challenge

Try spreading the columns further apart to see how well the cables work. Or try using different materials for the bridge deck. Can you get a paper deck to hold traffic? Do cables help? Do you need more or fewer cables?

CHAPTER 4

FOUNDATIONS

All structures need a solid base, or foundation, to stay strong. Structural foundations are like the roots of a tree. They are usually hidden below ground. But they are enormous and very important.

Concrete, wood and steel are commonly used to build foundations.

SOIL STRENGTH

Few structures are built on solid rock. Most are built on soil or span over water. Some soils are strong and firm. Others, such as sand, are weaker. The best soils for building on have a good mix of clay and different sizes of rock. But even strong soils can lose their strength when they get wet. Have you ever walked across the park after heavy rain? Did you notice how much more your feet sank into the wet ground than they do in dry soil? Imagine how much more that soil shifts under the weight of a large skyscraper.

Changes in temperature can also change the strength of the soil. Foundations must reach deep below winter frost. Frozen ground expands. It can cause a structure to shift and crack.

Before building a structure, engineers study soil samples from the site. They determine the soil strength. Soil is layered. Often the soil a couple of metres underground is different from soil near the surface. Drilling deep into the ground, engineers remove samples from all the soil layers. They use these samples to determine soil strength.

Engineers take multiple soil samples all around a building site before construction begins.

FOOTINGS

Soil strength determines the foundation type. Foundations are usually made from concrete. Concrete is strong. It is easy to place under structures. It also provides a heavy base for a building.

Concrete footings support many buildings. Footings are slabs that are larger than the column or wall placed on them. The footing spreads out the structure's weight over a larger area. Footings work like snowshoes or surfboards. When trying to stand on snow or water, your weight pushes you through the surface. But a snowshoe or surfboard spreads out your weight. Then water or snow can support your weight. The weaker the soil, the larger the footing needs to be to spread out a building's weight.

spread footing

Another type of footing is a pier. Piers are large columns of concrete beneath a structure. They are useful when building on very weak soil. Piers extend deep into the ground to rest on stronger soil or rock layers below.

pier foundation

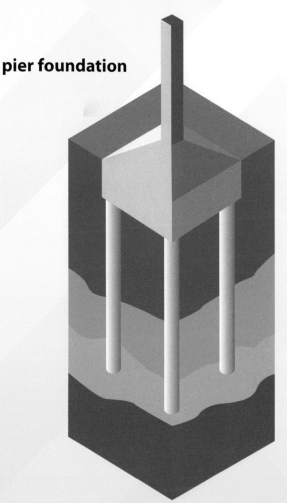

LEANING TOWER OF PISA

Have you seen photos of the Leaning Tower of Pisa? It is a famous example of the soil's effect on a structure. This 56-metre (185-foot) tower was built in Pisa, Italy, in the 1300s. It has an obvious tilt. The soil under one side of the building compresses more than the soil on the other side. The imbalance causes the heavy tower to lean.

EXPERIMENT WITH SOIL STRENGTHS AND FOUNDATIONS

Do you want to see how different soil conditions affect footing and pier strength? You can, with just a few common items from your kitchen.

MATERIALS

PUFFED RICE CEREAL

4 SOUP TINS

WATER

SMALL ROASTING TIN

3 CORKS

13-CENTIMETRE (5-INCH) SQUARE PIECE OF CORRUGATED CARDBOARD

STEPS

1   Pour 4 centimetres (1.5 inches) of cereal into the roasting tin. Level the cereal so it is flat.

2   Put a soup tin on the cereal. Keep stacking tins until they begin to tilt.

2

4

8

3   Remove the tins and re-level the cereal. Place the cardboard in the centre of the roasting tin.

4   Now stack tins on the cardboard footing until they begin to tilt. Does the footing make the tower of tins more stable?

5   Remove the tins and cardboard. Slowly pour water into the cereal until it is mostly wet.

6   Now try stacking tins on the wet "soil".

7   Try placing the cardboard on the wet cereal and stacking cans on it. What happens?

8   Remove the tins. Place three corks into the wet cereal like piers. Now stack tins on the corks. Can you stack more tins?

WHAT HAPPENED?

In this project you experimented with wet and dry soil and two different types of foundations. The cardboard footing helped spread the weight of the tins so that the cereal could hold more of them. You also saw that wet soil can be even weaker. Piers worked well with wet soil.

Challenge

Try using different types of cereal to see if the soil strength changes. Also try using a thicker or wider piece of cardboard for the footing. Is a bigger or thicker footing stronger?

CHAPTER 5

HORIZONTAL SYSTEMS

Sometimes structures have pieces that seem to go in many directions. They may look like their design doesn't make sense. However, each piece is part of a system. And each system is designed for a special purpose.

The horizontal structural system is the first system that engineers think about. It supports roofs and floors. It carries their weight to the vertical system. Then the vertical system connects to the foundation.

BEAMS AND JOISTS

The main horizontal structural pieces are beams and joists. Beams are usually solid pieces of steel, wood or concrete. Joists are made from smaller pieces of steel or wood. They are usually connected in a series of triangular patterns.

Beams and joists face bending forces. They are usually pulled by tension at the bottom and pushed by compression at the top. Smaller beams often span between beams and joists. They hold the wood or steel decking that supports the floors and roof of a building.

GLULAM

A special wood-based material is used for beams in some structures. Glulam is a material made from wood pieces tightly glued together. Glulams are stronger than ordinary wood. They can be made bigger to span further and carry more weight.

REINFORCED CONCRETE

A system of beams and decking is often seen in steel and wooden buildings. But large concrete slabs are used in some horizontal systems. Concrete slabs can be shaped with ridges. The ridges act like built-in beams. A concrete slab can do all the work of the beams and deck in a single piece.

Concrete is a good building material for structures that are exposed to weather or water. It is commonly used for multi-storey car parks and indoor swimming pools. Concrete doesn't rust like steel or rot like wood. But concrete has very little strength in tension and cracks easily. So how do concrete structures stand up? Concrete is almost never used alone as a structural material. Steel is strong in compression and tension. Steel reinforcing bars are inside each concrete slab or beam. These steel bars help withstand tension forces. Together the concrete and reinforcing bars are called reinforced concrete.

steel reinforced concrete beams

homogeneous made of parts or elements that are all the same

MATERIAL PROPERTIES

Steel is a **homogeneous** material. That means it has the same properties throughout. Wood is a **heterogeneous** material. It has different properties throughout. Wood is stronger in one direction than the other because of the way trees grow. Concrete is a mixture of water, cement powder and small rocks. This mixture is called a **composite** material.

heterogeneous made of parts and elements of different kinds that are from the same source

composite made up of many parts from different sources

PROJECT 5

MAKE YOUR OWN REINFORCED CONCRETE

You can use some common ingredients to see how reinforced concrete beams work.

MATERIALS

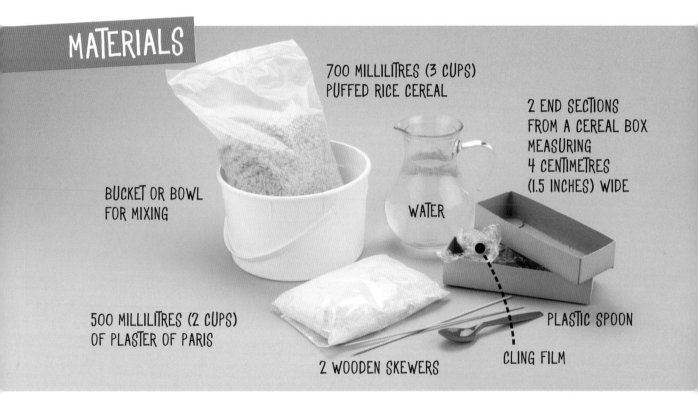

700 MILLILITRES (3 CUPS) PUFFED RICE CEREAL

2 END SECTIONS FROM A CEREAL BOX MEASURING 4 CENTIMETRES (1.5 INCHES) WIDE

BUCKET OR BOWL FOR MIXING

WATER

500 MILLILITRES (2 CUPS) OF PLASTER OF PARIS

PLASTIC SPOON

2 WOODEN SKEWERS

CLING FILM

STEPS

I Line the cardboard box sections with cling film. These will be the moulds for your concrete beam.

30

2 Use the pointed end of a skewer to punch two holes in the short side of one of the boxes about 2 centimetres (0.75 inches) from its bottom. Make the holes about 2 centimetres (0.75 inches) apart.

3 Make holes in the same place at the opposite end of the box.

4 Stick a skewer into each of the holes, through the cling film and across the box.

5 Quickly stir together the plaster and 200 millilitres (1 cup) of water until smooth.

6 Add the cereal. Mix quickly and evenly. This is your "concrete".

7 Spread the wet concrete evenly into both of the box ends. Pack it down tightly.

8 Let the "concrete beams" harden for at least 30 minutes.

9 Carefully remove them from the moulds.

10 Hold the beam without skewers between your hands. Push on it with your thumbs to bend it slowly until it breaks.

11 Now test the reinforced beam by bending it in the same way.

WHAT HAPPENED?

The plaster and water harden like real cement. It holds the cereal pieces together the way cement holds rocks in concrete. The skewers act like reinforcing bars. When you bend the beam, the skewers keep it from breaking.

CHAPTER 6

VERTICAL SYSTEMS

A vertical system brings loads from the horizontal system to the foundation. Walls and columns are parts of vertical systems.

Columns are solid pieces of steel, concrete or wood. They go from floor to ceiling, from floor to floor. Columns attach to beams at each level. They are often hidden inside walls. But they can be seen inside large open buildings.

Columns and walls usually face compression forces. But unevenly loaded columns undergo both compression and bending. You will have seen uneven loading if you've ever stacked wooden blocks. When the blocks are balanced you can stack them high. But if blocks are placed slightly off centre, the stack shifts. It eventually falls. When a column shifts to one side and falls, engineers call it buckling.

Some buildings, such as stadiums, must be completely open. They must have no columns inside. In this case, frames are used. In a frame, beams and columns are connected together with special heavy-duty connections. The beams and columns work together in a shape similar to an arch.

BEIJING'S BIRD'S NEST

China's 91,000-seat National Stadium was built for the 2008 Olympics. It is nicknamed "The Bird's Nest". The stadium was designed to look like a type of Chinese pottery that has cracked glazing. The structural pieces supporting the stadium look random. But they are actually a series of carefully designed and engineered overlapping steel frames that support the structure.

EXPERIMENT WITH COLUMNS

Build columns of different shapes and lengths. Test them out to see what shapes and sizes are strongest.

MATERIALS

7 SHEETS OF PAPER 20 X 25 CENTIMETRES (8 X 10 INCHES)

CLEAR TAPE

SCISSORS

SEVERAL PAPERBACK BOOKS FOR STACKING

STEPS

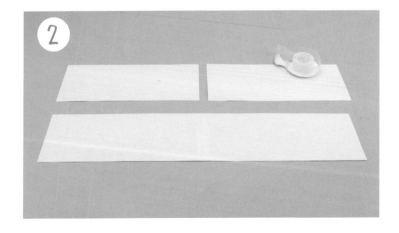

1 Cut each piece of paper in half lengthways.

2 Lay two of these pieces end-to-end. Tape them together to make a longer piece.

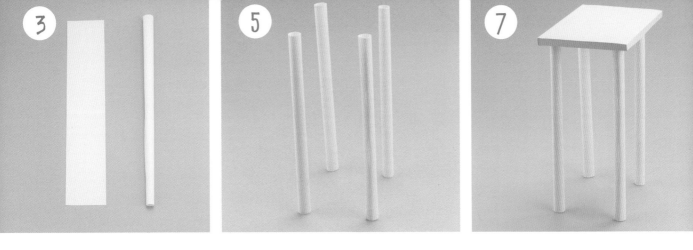

3   Roll this piece into a long tube that is 3 centimetres (1 inch) in diameter. Tape it securely. Make sure the ends are flat and even by standing the column up.

4   Repeat Steps 2 and 3 to make three more long columns.

5   Roll and tape four of the remaining paper halves into columns that are 3 centimetres (1 inch) in diameter. This will make four medium-length columns.

6   Cut the remaining paper halves in half widthways. Roll and tape these pieces into tubes to make four short columns.

7   Stand the four long columns in a square. Gently place a book across the columns. Keep stacking books until the columns buckle.

8   Stack books on the medium columns and the short columns. See how many each can hold. What do you notice?

WHAT HAPPENED?

Notice that the longer columns buckle under less weight than shorter ones. Engineers attach long columns to floors or walls. Doing this spreads the load out into smaller sections and stops the columns buckling.

Challenge

Try the experiment using square or triangular shaped columns. Do they perform the same way? Does the material matter? What if you make the columns from cardboard? Try filling the columns with sand. Does this make them stronger?

CHAPTER 7

LATERAL SYSTEMS

Is it possible to feel seasick hundreds of metres in the air? That's what some people feel like in very tall skyscrapers. These buildings can sway a few metres in strong winds. Wind forces are planned for when engineers design buildings. So are earthquake tremors. Both forces can sway or shake a building side-to-side. These sideways loads are called lateral loads. Each structure must have a system for resisting lateral loads.

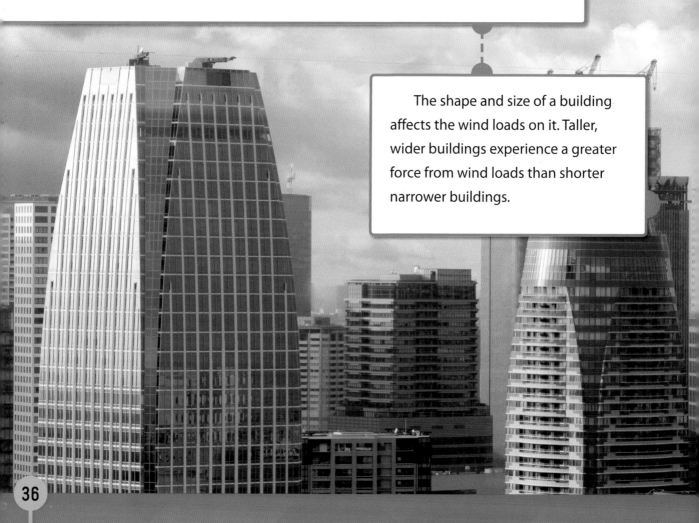

The shape and size of a building affects the wind loads on it. Taller, wider buildings experience a greater force from wind loads than shorter narrower buildings.

SHANGHAI WORLD FINANCIAL CENTER

The Shanghai World Financial Center in Shanghai, China, is one of the world's tallest skyscrapers. It was designed with a large hole near its top. The hole allows wind to rush through, relieving wind forces on the building.

Wind blowing on tall buildings also affects lower buildings nearby. People in the streets around them are affected too. Like a giant sail, a skyscraper changes the wind's direction. When a gust hits a tall building, the air swirls down to street level. Engineers must consider this effect when designing new skyscrapers.

BRACES AND SHEAR WALLS

Certain structural parts gather lateral loads. They pass these forces to the foundation. The easiest lateral system to see is bracing. Braces are small pieces of criss-crossing metal. The braces make the shape of Xs or Ks between columns. Some tall buildings may look like they are made of glass, but they have bracing hidden behind the glass panels.

A building's walls, roofs or floors can also be part of its lateral system. A wall that is part of a lateral system is called a shear wall. Shear walls have special connections that help them carry lateral loads.

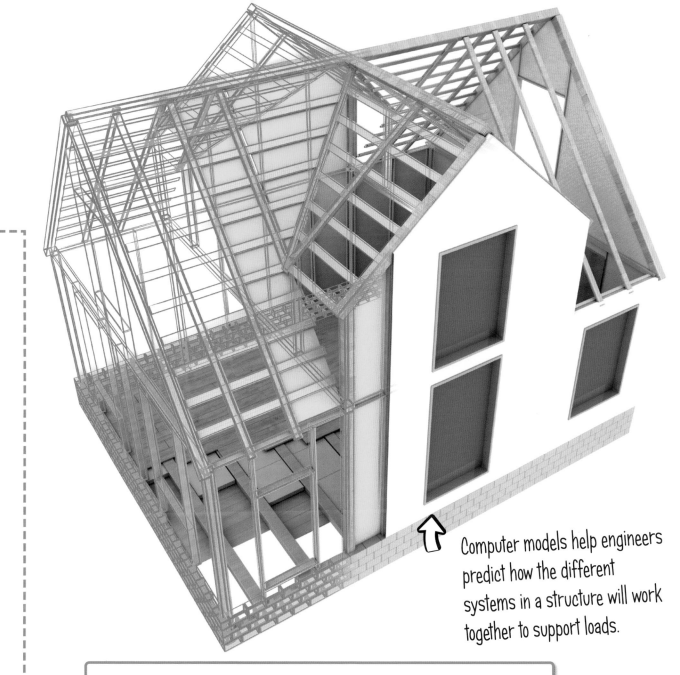

Computer models help engineers predict how the different systems in a structure will work together to support loads.

Engineers always think about **efficiency** when designing structures. Sometimes walls, roofs or floors are designed as part of more than one system. Engineers use computer models to design an entire structure. They apply the live loads and dead loads that a building may face to the model. Doing this allows them to determine the forces on each part of the building. They can then choose the correct material and size for each piece of the structure.

efficiency ability to do something well without wasted energy

EARTHQUAKE ENGINEERING

Buildings in earthquake areas are built to resist the shaking forces of an earthquake. Most buildings will be damaged in an earthquake. However, special systems can help prevent a building from failing entirely.

A base isolation system is used under some buildings. It allows a building to move with an earthquake to prevent it from breaking. In a base isolation system the building is built on plates called **bearings**. Bearings are made from rubber or lead. These materials are elastic enough to stretch and move with an earthquake. They slowly return to their original position afterwards.

A tuned mass damper is another earthquake system. It is a heavy weight hung from an upper storey of a building. When earthquake waves ripple through the base of the building the force is transferred from the building to the mass damper. The heavy weight swings. The swinging counteracts the earthquake forces to keep the building stable.

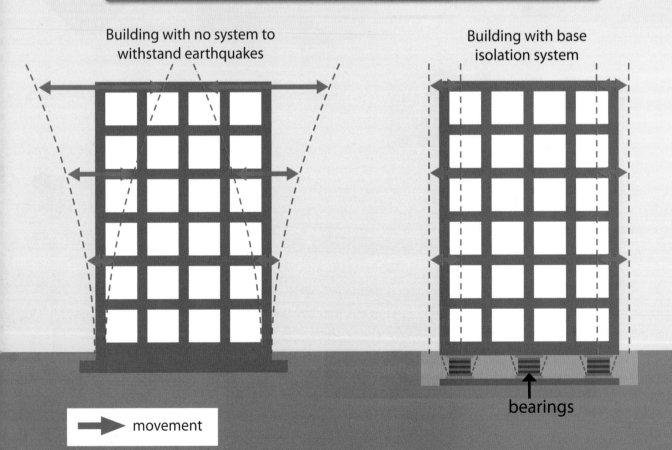

Building with no system to withstand earthquakes

Building with base isolation system

bearings

➡ movement

TAIPEI 101 MASS DAMPER

Taipei 101 in Taiwan is one of the tallest buildings in the world. Between its 87th and 92nd floor a 660-tonne globe hangs. This giant mass damper sways back and forth by up to 1 metre (3 feet). It stabilizes the building during typhoon gusts and earthquake tremors.

bearing pads of lead or rubber used as part of a base isolation system

EXPERIMENT WITH LATERAL LOADS

You can use some items from your kitchen to build your own tower.
Then test it for wind loads and earthquake forces.

MATERIALS

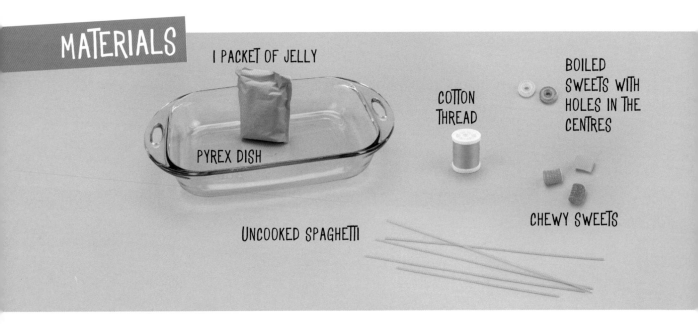

I PACKET OF JELLY

PYREX DISH

COTTON THREAD

BOILED SWEETS WITH HOLES IN THE CENTRES

CHEWY SWEETS

UNCOOKED SPAGHETTI

STEPS

1   Break two pieces of spaghetti in half. Arrange the pieces to form a square. Use a chewy sweet at each corner to hold the square together.

2   Repeat Step 1 to make two more squares.

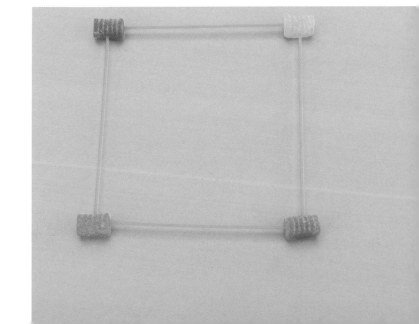

3 Break four pieces of spaghetti long enough to span the diagonal length of one of the squares you've made. Use them to make an "X" across two squares. You should have two squares with diagonals and one without.

4 Break 2.5 centimetres (1 inch) from the ends of four pieces of spaghetti.

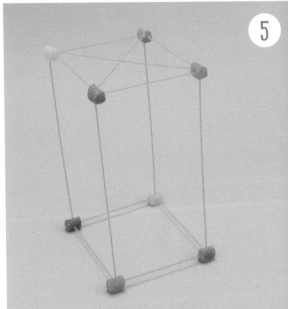

5 Place the square without diagonals on a table. Use the pieces of spaghetti to make columns. The columns will connect this square to one of the other square pieces.

6 Repeat Step 4 to make four more columns.

7 Use these columns to build another storey onto your tower, using the final square at the top.

8 Push sideways on one top corner of the tower. What happens?

9 Use full-length pieces of spaghetti to make "X" braces between some of the columns. Test the tower by pushing sideways again. How many braces do you need to make the tower resist the force?

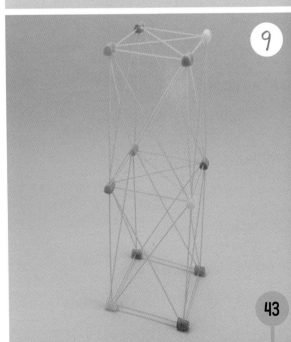

10   To test for earthquake forces, prepare the jelly according to the instructions on the packet. Pour it into the pyrex dish and refrigerate until it is set.

11   Put the tower on the jelly. Quickly shake the dish back and forth to produce an "earthquake". How stable is the tower? Remove the tower from the jelly.

12 Thread one boiled sweet onto a piece of cotton, and hang it from the centre of the top "X". Let the sweet hang down about 8 centimetres (3 inches) from the top of the tower.

13 Repeat Step 12, but tie the sweet to the middle "X". The sweets are your mass dampers.

14 Place the tower back on the jelly. Shake it as before. Do your mass dampers counteract your "earthquake" forces?

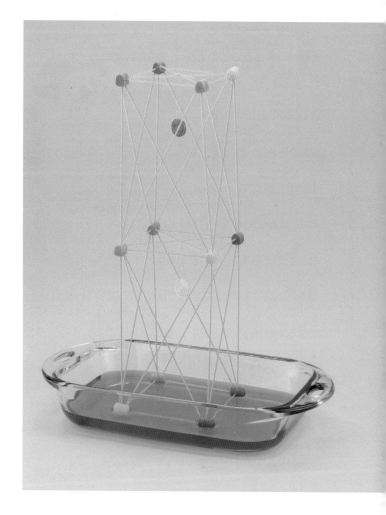

WHAT HAPPENED?

In this project you experimented with two different lateral systems. The X-bracing gave the structure support against sideways forces. When the tower experienced wave-like tremors, the hanging sweets supplied the counterbalance. They kept the tower standing, much like the mass dampers used in skyscrapers.

Structural engineers are responsible for innovations such as mass dampers. Continue experimenting with structural engineering and you may build the structures of the future!

GLOSSARY

abutment   concrete support at the end of a bridge

bearing   pads of lead or rubber used as part of a base isolation system

composite   made up of many parts from different sources

compression   pushing force

deck   part of a bridge that people walk or drive on

deflection   small changes in the shape of a structure

efficiency   ability to do something well without wasted energy

elasticity   ability of something to change shape and then return to its original shape

heterogeneous   made of parts and elements of different kinds that are from the same source

homogeneous   made of parts or elements that are all the same

resist   oppose or slow the motion of an object

superstructure   part of a bridge that supports the deck

tension   pulling force

torsion   twisting force

READ MORE

Buildings (Design and Engineering), Alex Woolf (Raintree, 2014)

Buildings and Structures (Sci-Hi: Science and Technology), Andrew Solway (Raintree, 2011)

See Inside Famous Buildings (Usborne See Inside), Rob Lloyd Jones (Usborne Publishing Ltd, 2009)

WEBSITES

www.bbc.co.uk/guides/zqyr9j6
Learn more about how skyscrapers are built and how they remain standing.

www.dkfindout.com/uk/history/ancient-rome/roman-buildings/
Find out more about ancient Roman engineering.

INDEX

AUTHOR BIO

Tammy Enz holds a bachelor's degree in Civil Engineering and a master's degree in Journalism and Mass Communications. She teaches at the University of Wisconsin-Platteville in the United States and has written several science and engineering books for young people. Her "Invent It" series was awarded *Learning Magazine*'s 2013 Teachers' Choice Awards for the Family and she co-authored Capstone's Batman Science series, recipient of a 2015 Science Communication Award from the American Institute of Physics. She lives in Wisconsin with her husband and two children.